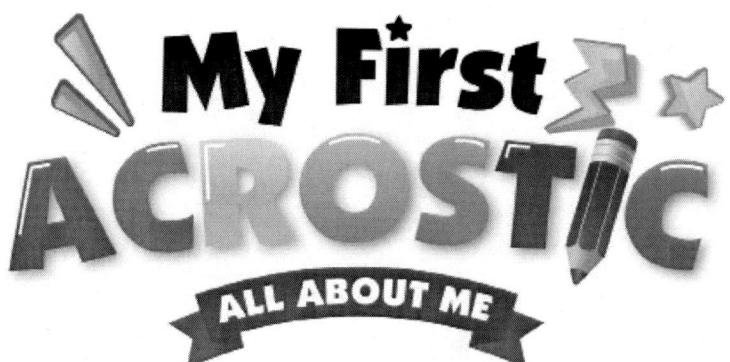

Awesome Acrostics

Edited By Holly Sheppard

First published in Great Britain in 2020 by:

Young Writers
Remus House
Coltsfoot Drive
Peterborough
PE2 9BF
Telephone: 01733 890066
Website: www.youngwriters.co.uk

Printed and bound in the UK by BookPrintingUK
Website: www.bookprintinguk.com
YB0430A

Dear Reader,

Welcome to a fun-filled book of acrostic poems!

Here at Young Writers, we are delighted to introduce our new poetry competition for KS1 pupils, *My First Acrostic: All About Me*. Acrostic poems are an enjoyable way to introduce pupils to the world of poetry and allow the young writer to open their imagination to a range of topics of their choice. The colourful and engaging entry forms allowed even the youngest (or most reluctant) of pupils to create a poem using the acrostic technique, and with that, encouraged them to include other literary techniques such as similes and description. Here at Young Writers we are passionate about introducing the love and art of creative writing to the next generation and we love being a part of their journey.

From pets to family, from hobbies to idols, these pupils have shaped and crafted their ideas brilliantly, showcasing their budding creativity. So, we invite you to proceed through these pages and take a glimpse into these blossoming young writers' minds. We hope you will relish these poems as much as we have.

Contents

Conrad Morgan (6) 52
Nevaeh Rose Carrington (6) 53
Connor Ditch (6) 54
Katie Julian (6) 55
Shamsa Eid (6) 56
Ronnie O'Connor (7) 57
Elivea-Mae Dyson (7) 58
Freya Atkinson (6) 59
Mia Ma (6) 60
Charlie Addy (6) 61
Harry Kirk (6) 62
Poppy Baxter (6) 63
Alex Brownlow (6) 64
Amelie Siddall (7) 65
Cherry-Eve Towner-Mudd (6) 66
Aiden Chambers (7) 67
Betsy Binns (7) 68
Isaac Walvin (6) 69
Oscar James Moore (6) 70
Coby Joe Gerrard Kilgour (6) 71
Seth Knight (6) 72
Toby Bradley (6) 73
Eli Newton (6) 74

East Claydon School, East Claydon

Lucy Probets (6) 75
Amélie Prudhomme (6) 76
Luna Mae Price (6) 77
Maisie McIvor (6) 78

Fingringhoe CE Primary School, Fingringhoe

Remy Lenehan (7) 79
Samuel Dilliway (7) 80
Poppy Cockram (6) 81
Alessandro Asioli (6) 82
Renesmay Willsher (6) 83
Millie Kay Jones (6) 84
Charlie Walker (6) 85

Grove CE Primary School, Grove

Lily Leigh Wells (9) 86
Olivia Dalgleish (10) 87
Megan Zamora Rowe (9) 88
Benny Stoten (9) 89
Eleanor-May Woodley (7) 90
Jack Perkins (9) 91
Charlotte Lily Dalgleish (7) 92
Beth Barnes (7) 93
George Mowatt (7) 94
Justin James Harvey 95
Mathieson (7)
Annabeth Manton (7) 96
Morgan Niblett (8) 97
Summer Langley (8) 98
Megan Hackwood (9) 99
Keira Kelly (6) 100
Naila Amonua Amoa-Sakyi (9) 101
Isaac Mattam (7) 102
Phoebe Hackwood (7) 103

Limehurst Community Primary School, Limehurst Village

Evie Whitehouse (6) 104
Noah James Bowden (6) 105

St Joseph's Catholic Primary School, Aldershot

Cameron Poulsom (4) 106
Mary McGinty (4) 107
Ava Campbell (4) 108
Olivia Norman (4) 109
Eli Barclay (4) 110
Zuzanna Witoslaw (4) 111
Ava-Mary Eldred (4) 112
Andreea Vlad (4) 113

Stickney CE Primary School, Stickney

Emily Ann Falby (7) 114
Karlie Benton (6) 115

Isla Clarke (6)	116
Reggie Waterson (6)	117
Jake Toin (6)	118
Amelia Patching (6)	119
Logan Diamond (7)	120
Max Morbey (7)	121
Adele Smith (6)	122
Valentina Smith (6)	123

West Kirby Primary School, West Kirby

James Howell (7)	124
Tabby Simpson (6)	125
Matthew Kerwick (6)	126
Charlotte Rowland (6)	127
Philip McCormick (6)	128

The Poems

Mathematics

M aths is magnificent

A ddition is my addiction

T elling the time uses maths

H istory has lots of famous mathematicians

E very day I do maths

M any scientists need maths

A stronauts need maths to get back to Earth

T aking away is subtraction

I nfinity is never-ending

C alculators are machines

S anta needs maths to deliver presents.

Axel Kismat Kyriacou (6)

Ashford Park Primary School, Ashford

Family

F ingers so tiny, smaller than a crayon
A nimals on his clothes, the lion is called Leon
M y brother cries a lot, *wah-wah*, so loud
I magine me, a big sister, I am very proud
L ittle baby brother, his name is Ralph
Y ucky, he is sick a lot, coming from his mouth.

Ruby Steel (6)
Ashford Park Primary School, Ashford

Unicorns

U niorns are magical
N othing I love more
I would love to ride a unicorn
C hloe would call her sparkle
O nly special people see them
R iding through the sky
N ow close your eyes and make a wish, you
might see one too.

Chloe Sophia Knowles (7)
Ashford Park Primary School, Ashford

Friendly Unicorn

U mbrellas are for rain and when it's too hot

N uts are for everyone but not in school

I love my mum and dad

C ats are my favourite animal

O ats are my favourite

R oses are the best

N isha is my best friend.

Benisha Yadav (6)

Ashford Park Primary School, Ashford

Family

F amily means everything to me
A lways make me laugh, hee hee hee
M illions of memories on holidays
I love my family in so many ways
L iving with them is like a dream
Y um yum, we always eat ice cream.

Jaxon Allen (6)
Ashford Park Primary School, Ashford

Purse

P ennies are kept in it

U mbrellas protect them from getting wet

R ing the police if it is stolen

S unlight makes it shine

E ndangered animals' skin shouldn't be used to make them.

Adwait Sawke (6)

Ashford Park Primary School, Ashford

Autumn

A pples falling off the tree

U nder my feet they crunch

T he leaf falls on the tiger

U mbrella is getting covered in apples and leaves

M oney is under the red leaves

N uts under the leaves and apples.

Finlay Brown (11)

Barndale House School, Alnwick

Autumn

A utumn is here

U nder the ground potatoes, carrots and radishes grow

T he leaves are falling

U nder the leaf on the grass is a squirrel

M um likes autumn

N ext to my friend is an autumn tree.

JJ Turnbull (11)
Barndale House School, Alnwick

Autumn

A pples fall off the tree
U nder the tree is a conker
T he leaves are falling down
U nderground the carrots grow
M uddy, cold water
N oise of two loud cows mooing.

Liam Wilson (10)

Barndale House School, Alnwick

Autumn

A utumn is my favourite time of the year
U mbrellas everywhere
T oast
U mbrella
M y favourite colour is red like a leaf
N ext to the orange leaf.

Lucy Philomena Hunter (11)
Barndale House School, Alnwick

Mummy

M y mum Jane

U nderstands me well

M ummy is so pretty

M erlot is her favourite wine

Y ummy scrummy is my mummy.

Molly Rutter (19)

Barndale House School, Alnwick

Buster

B oisterous Buster

U p high

S illy boy

T roublemaker

E nergetic

R uns around and around.

Levi Taylor (18)

Barndale House School, Alnwick

Dolphins

D id you know that I splash in the sea?

O nly dolphins can click, whistle, dive and grunt

L ove to eat fish

P lease take care of us

H ow many teeth? Ninety-eight sharp, peg teeth

I follow boats

N ot keen on chips to go with my fish

S quid is my favourite food.

Willow Hayman (5)

Bedstone College, Bedstone

Summer Rose

S ummer is my name
U nicorns are my favourite
M ummy is my best friend
M ice go *squeak squeak*
E ating is my favourite thing to do
R eading books every night.

R eally funny I am
O reo is my cat's name
S eeing my cousin Isla I love
E very day I draw.

Summer Douglas (5)

Brook Street Primary School, Carlisle

Mateusz

M y nickname is Mati
A lways a good boy
T he dog Mopi is my best friend
E very day I love to play football
U sually I go to bed at 8pm
S trawberry is my favourite fruit
Z oo is my favourite place.

Mateusz Piotrowski (5)

Brook Street Primary School, Carlisle

Super Rainbows

R ight across the sky
A lways pretty to see
I love them
N ow I've seen a rainbow
B eautiful and bright
O range is the best
W onderful rainbows.

Ella Broome (5)
Brook Street Primary School, Carlisle

Friends

F unny games are the best
R eading stories
I laugh with them
E ating sweets
N atalie's my best friend
D ays are fantastic
S he loves me.

Lena Maria Szpurgis (5)
Brook Street Primary School, Carlisle

Batman

B ad guys are afraid
A cape waves in the air
T o the Batmobile
M oving fast
A true hero
N ever fails.

Noah Zajac (5)
Brook Street Primary School, Carlisle

April Edwards

A pril is my name
P ink and purple are my favourite colours
R oses are my favourite flowers
I sla is my best friend
L aurie-Aver is my best friend.

E lephants are my favourite animals
D arcie is my best friend
W innie and Wilbur is my favourite book
A t Halloween it scares me
R iley is my best friend
D ylan is my best friend
S ophie is my best friend forever.

April Edwards (6)
Clowne Infant & Nursery School, Clowne

Marvellous Me

M e and Sophie wanted to plant pink and yellow flowers but our teacher wouldn't let us

A lways when I come to school, I have a little laugh

D aisie and I like to play games together

D ifferent days I come to school and I have a little fun

I f you have a brother, you may fight

S ometimes you can do something silly but it might be so funny

O n Friday, it is so fun

N ow I am in Year Two I know what to do.

Maddison Anders (7)

Clowne Infant & Nursery School, Clowne

All About Me

I sla is my name and I really like it.

S aturday, I go and play on my phone.

L et's go and laugh all the time.

A nd I always eat apples for my tea.

G irls love playing in my garden, it's fun.

O ctober is my special day, it's my birthday.

U nder my bed is messy. I use a ruler to measure.

G osh, my house is a happy place I love.

H ome, it is comfy to be there.

Isla Rose Gough (7)

Clowne Infant & Nursery School, Clowne

Kai Anders

K ai is the best because he is a good friend

A nd my favourite game is Sonic Boom

I n my house I have a great family

A nd my sisters are called Abigayle and Maddison

N oah is my best friend in school

D arcie and Dylan are in my class

E ve is in Class Three

R iley and Ronnie are my best friends

S anta is special because he gives you presents in December.

Kai Anders (7)

Clowne Infant & Nursery School, Clowne

Laurie-Aver Cambell

L aurie-Aver is my name and I really like it
A nd my favourite animal is an okapi
U nder my bed it is always a mess
R unning is my favourite exercise
I like cats, they're cute
E lisabeth is my best friend.

A pril is my very best friend
V ery happy to be in Mr Livesey's class
E veryone is my best friend
R unning is good exercise.

Laurie-Aver Cambell (7)
Clowne Infant & Nursery School, Clowne

My Name Is Noah

N oah is my name
O n a Sunday, I go to my grandma's for dinner
A piece of jelly can make me poorly
H i, my name is Noah and I like playing football.

S mith is my second name
M y dad's name is Dean
I n my house, I have an eighty-five inch TV
T he Christmas bells get us very excited
H i, I'm Noah's mum, Noah is a great boy!

Noah Smith (7)
Clowne Infant & Nursery School, Clowne

All About Me

A lex is my name and everyone likes it
L aughs are fun with me
E verybody likes to play with me
X ylophone is my favourite instrument.

T hirteen is my favourite number
U nder jungles, I like to see anacondas
R ed is my favourite colour
N ight-time is my favourite time
E very day I go to school
R oses are my favourite flower.

Alex Turner (6)
Clowne Infant & Nursery School, Clowne

Marvellous Me

N ever go to sleep when my parents tell me and I can't get to sleep in the middle of the night

I 'm important because I have spots on the back of my legs

C aring for you and me are my family

O utside in the fresh air I like to play

L ying down on my soft bed, shutting my eyes and going to sleep

E very day I say Mrs Galley is the best teacher.

Nicole Hart (7)
Clowne Infant & Nursery School, Clowne

Marvellous Me

S ome people call me Soph, I really don't know why

O f all the teddies in my room, my rainbow bear is the best out of them all

P ink is one of my favourite colours and it fills me with joy

H ave me as your sister because I am the nicest girl you can meet

I have the nicest friends and the teacher

E verywhere I go, I think about my dream pet.

Sophie Lardeaux (6)

Clowne Infant & Nursery School, Clowne

My Adventures

R iley is my name
I live in Clowne
L eapfrogs are my favourite animal
E very day I go to the gym and lift weights
Y esterday I went home to my nan's.

H is the first letter in my last name
A t the park, we always play
R abbits are my favourite animals
T ea is at three o'clock at night.

Riley Hart (7)
Clowne Infant & Nursery School, Clowne

All About Me

A nnabella is my name

N ever go to the zoo ever again

N umbers are my favourite

A pril is my best friend

B ella is my name

E lephants are my favourite animals

L aurie-Aver is my friend too because she is friends with my other friend

L azy day on Sunday, I just sit and play

A pples are my favourite.

Annabella-Rose Greveson
Clowne Infant & Nursery School, Clowne

Freddy

F ood is my favourite because I like chicken curry

R ain is bad in school because you get wet play

E lephants are the best because they have big trunks

D rawing is the best activity because you get to colour in at the end

D ogs are the best because they have nice hair

Y es, I do want pasta for my tea, Daddy and Mummy.

Freddy Peacock (6)

Clowne Infant & Nursery School, Clowne

Marvellous Me

E very day I go to school

V ery long are the six hours

E ve, some people call me Evie.

C harlotte is one of my BFFs

A nd my favourite fruits are apples and strawberries

N o littering, I hate littering

D addy loves green, that is his favourite colour

Y ou are my friends, all of you.

Eve Candy (6)

Clowne Infant & Nursery School, Clowne

All About Me

L eo is is my name
E ggs are nice
O ranges are my favourite.

L emons are sour
E ggs are yummy foods
V ery scared of big spiders
E nglish is fun
S wimming is good
L ovely pears are sweet
E ggs have yolk in it
Y es, I like oranges.

Leo Levesley (6)
Clowne Infant & Nursery School, Clowne

All About Me

G eorgia is my name and I like gold
E lephants are my favourite, I love them. Every night I wish I had one!
O striches are funny and cute
R ebecca is my best friend forever
G rason is my best friend
I love Conrad, he is my boyfriend
A lex Brownlow is funny.

Georgia Perry-Clark (6)
Clowne Infant & Nursery School, Clowne

All About Me

On **T** uesdays I go to my granma's and I
surprise her

H oliday, I go to Cornwall and I have lots
and lots of fun

O n my TV I watch YouTube all day

M onkeys are my favourite animal and I
love apples to eat

A nd I can be silly a bit

S ometimes I get bored.

Thomas Freddie Jack Else (6)
Clowne Infant & Nursery School, Clowne

Marvellous Me

A ll people call me Arch but Freddy calls me Archie

R ain is bad because we don't have playtime

C harlotte is one of my best friends

H arry is my best friend

I am Archie and I love my mum, dad and my brother

E ngland is the best team in the world.

Archie King (6)

Clowne Infant & Nursery School, Clowne

Marvellous Me

J essica is a child who's got a big smile
E veryone is my friend, even the teacher
S o I like my family and me
S o I like to show my new look
I like to play on my own
C adance is my best friend
A pples are yummy, I like apples.

Jessica Butler (6)
Clowne Infant & Nursery School, Clowne

All About Me

S carlett is my name

C ycling is my favourite thing

A nd I like walking

R unning is best

L ots of cuddly teddies

E very day I like to eat chocolate cake

T oday, I ate chocolate cake

T omorrow I will eat chocolate cake.

Scarlett Lee (6)

Clowne Infant & Nursery School, Clowne

My Life

R egan is my name, yoga is my entertainment
E ntering my house, loving my puppy more
G reen is my favourite colour, same as red
A nd instead of that, my favourite drink is a milkshake
N odding my head is me but I do brush my teeth for hygiene.

Regan Kelly-Brown (7)
Clowne Infant & Nursery School, Clowne

Marvellous Me

A ll of Class Three are the best at writing
M rs Galley is a good teacher
E yes are good because you can see thing
L ooked at a plant yesterday
I nsects I like because there are lots of them
In **A** ugust, I am going on holiday.

Amelia Welton (7)

Clowne Infant & Nursery School, Clowne

Poem About Magic Me

L ucy is my name
U nicorns are the best toys ever
C ycling is a good exercise for you
Y ellow is an amazing colour.

T eachers work very hard
E very day I learn at school
E njoying things make me smile.

Lucy Florence Tee (6)
Clowne Infant & Nursery School, Clowne

My Cool Acrostic

J ozef is my name, Roblox is my game

O n Roblox, all you do is play, play, play

Z ebras are my favourite animal, they are black and white

E lephants live in Africa, that's what I know

F earless is my nature, nothing scares me!

Jozef Kostewicz (6)

Clowne Infant & Nursery School, Clowne

Darcie

D arcie is my name, I like my name
A pples are my favourite fruit
R aspberries are my favourite fruit
C ream with jelly and ice cream is my favourite
I ce cream and ice lollies
E lephants are my favourite animals.

Darcie Goodlad (6)
Clowne Infant & Nursery School, Clowne

All About Me!

I care for Jesus and God

S ophie is my friend

A pples are my favourite

B utterflies are the best

E ggs are good for me

L ots of people like me

L ambs make me laugh

E lizabeth is my friend.

Isabelle Scarlett Askew (6)

Clowne Infant & Nursery School, Clowne

Marvellous Me

C ats are my favourite pets
A nd I like cheetahs and dinosaurs too
S ometimes I eat pizza
S weets are my best delicious treats
I like the colours purple and dark blue
E very Sunday, I go to swimming lessons.

Cassie Reynolds (6)
Clowne Infant & Nursery School, Clowne

Marvellous Me

C adance is playful
A nd I like playing with my pup
D aniel is my dad's name
A nd Cheryl is my mum's name
N ext, I like to go to the cinema
C risps are fun
E leven is my favourite number.

Cadance Ella Moore (6)

Clowne Infant & Nursery School, Clowne

Marvellous Me

G eorge is my name
E very day in September I am at school
O ften I don't work but I do
R acing is my favourite game
G oing into the garden to play is so fun
E verybody loves me in this class.

George Fisher (6)
Clowne Infant & Nursery School, Clowne

All About Me

C hloe is my name and I like it

H appy to play on my phone all day on Saturday

L ast week it was sunny, now it's raining

O utside, it was muddy on the grass

E veryone on my table is my friend.

Chloe Parker (6)

Clowne Infant & Nursery School, Clowne

Marvellous Me

P eyton is in Class Three
E veryone in this class is quiet
Y esterday it was raining outside
T oday it was not raining
O utside I play on the trampoline
N ow I have a new toy.

Peyton Hodkin (6)
Clowne Infant & Nursery School, Clowne

Callum

C allum is my name
A t school I do lots of work
L iving is wonderful
L ifting weights is good for me
U sing my football boots makes my feet comfy
M ondays are my favourite.

Callum Brown (6)

Clowne Infant & Nursery School, Clowne

All About Me

M onday I went on my bike
A nd an apple fell on my head
I 'm watching the moon with the
S tars
I saw a lion so I screamed
E very morning I have a warm, boiled egg.

Maisie Louise White (7)
Clowne Infant & Nursery School, Clowne

All About Me

J essica Rose Hudson is my name
E ve in Class Three is my friend
S eth is good
S ometimes
I play with Seth
C lowne is where I live
A good friend is nice.

Jessica Rose Hudson (6)
Clowne Infant & Nursery School, Clowne

All About Me

C ats are my favourite animals
O n the weekends I play
N othing makes me sad
R obins are my favourite birds
A pples are my favourite
D ogs are my favourite animals.

Conrad Morgan (6)

Clowne Infant & Nursery School, Clowne

Marvellous Me

N evaeh is my name

E dinburgh is my favourite place

V ets help my pet

A book is good to read out loud

E ggs are my favourite meal

H alloween is my favourite.

Nevaeh Rose Carrington (6)

Clowne Infant & Nursery School, Clowne

Connor

C onnor is my name

O n Saturday I go on the iPad

In N ovember I like to watch fireworks

N ew stuff in my room and toys

O n Sunday I relax

R onny is my friend.

Connor Ditch (6)

Clowne Infant & Nursery School, Clowne

All About Me

K ittens are my favourite animal
A lways I go to school
T ogether we make good friends
I love my dogs because they are so cute
E veryone is my friend because I am nice.

Katie Julian (6)

Clowne Infant & Nursery School, Clowne

Marvellous Me

S hamsa Eid is my name
H enna on my hands
A nd I love cats
M y favourite food is crisps
S asida Eid is my sister's name
A castle is my best place to go.

Shamsa Eid (6)
Clowne Infant & Nursery School, Clowne

All About Me

R unning is my favourite thing
O ranges are juicy fruits
N an is nicer than my dad
N an is the best person
I n my house my mum is so busy
E ating is great.

Ronnie O'Connor (7)

Clowne Infant & Nursery School, Clowne

Elivea

E livea is my name and I like it
L ola is my BFF
I like cats
V ans are my favourite vehicle
E lephants are my favourite
A pril is my best friend forever.

Elivea-Mae Dyson (7)
Clowne Infant & Nursery School, Clowne

Freya And Chocolate Cake

F reya is my name
R ainbows are my favourite thing
E ating chocolate cake is a delicious thing
Y esterday I was counting to one hundred
A bouncy ball I would like.

Freya Atkinson (6)

Clowne Infant & Nursery School, Clowne

All About Me

M ia is my name
I have pet fishes and I love them so much
A nd I like the beach.

M y favourite thing is donkey rides
A t the beach is where the ocean is.

Mia Ma (6)

Clowne Infant & Nursery School, Clowne

Marvellous Me

C harlie can bake buns
H ave a family
A nd I go to Ibiza
R unning fast is fun
L ego I can build
I go on my bike
E than is my best friend.

Charlie Addy (6)
Clowne Infant & Nursery School, Clowne

Marvellous Me

H arry is in Class Three
A fter school I go home and play
R unning on the playground is the best
R iding my bike is my favourite
Y ou can do a poo and so can I.

Harry Kirk (6)
Clowne Infant & Nursery School, Clowne

All About Me

P oppy is my name

O n Saturday I like cycling

P eople call me Pop

P ippa is my dog and she is brown and white

Y ellow is my favourite colour and pink is too.

Poppy Baxter (6)

Clowne Infant & Nursery School, Clowne

Alex

A lex is my name and it is the best

L ove my mum and dad because they give me toys

E veryone likes to play with me

X -rays are the best thing because they are clever.

Alex Brownlow (6)

Clowne Infant & Nursery School, Clowne

Amazing Amelie

A pples are nice

M y dog is a cockapoo

E xploring is my favourite thing

L ittle things I like

I play fun games

E arth is where I live.

Amelie Siddall (7)

Clowne Infant & Nursery School, Clowne

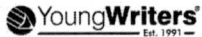

All About Me

C herry is my name
H am is my favourite food
E aster eggs
R achel is my mum's name
R ain is my favourite
Y es, I play outside.

Cherry-Eve Towner-Mudd (6)
Clowne Infant & Nursery School, Clowne

Aiden

A pple is my favourite fruit
I like going to school
D ark green is my favourite colour
E veryone plays with me
N ine is my favourite number.

Aiden Chambers (7)

Clowne Infant & Nursery School, Clowne

All About Me

B etsy is my name
E ating apples are the best
T igers are cute and great
S wimming is my favourite thing to do
Y ellow is nice for colouring.

Betsy Binns (7)

Clowne Infant & Nursery School, Clowne

Me

I like trains

S top Mum, you've crashed our car

A pples are my favourite food

A fter school, I go to Cubs

C hocolate cake is the best.

Isaac Walvin (6)

Clowne Infant & Nursery School, Clowne

Marvellous Me

O scar is a child who has a big smile
S miles a lot
C olouring is my favourite
A nd I go for swimming lessons
R ed is my favourite colour.

Oscar James Moore (6)
Clowne Infant & Nursery School, Clowne

Marvellous Me

C oby likes doing arts and crafts
O nly in the morning though
B ut Allanah likes Toy Story
Y ou and me have the best class ever.

Coby Joe Gerrard Kilgour (6)
Clowne Infant & Nursery School, Clowne

All About Me

S eth is my name and
E veryone likes it
T urtles are my favourite pets
H arry is my best friend, he plays with me.

Seth Knight (6)
Clowne Infant & Nursery School, Clowne

Marvellous Me

T oby is my name

O n Saturday, I play games

B ugs are my best pets

Y ellow is my favourite colour.

Toby Bradley (6)

Clowne Infant & Nursery School, Clowne

Eggs Are Best

E li likes eggs
L ike the tops
I like yo-yos.

Eli Newton (6)
Clowne Infant & Nursery School, Clowne

Autumn

A utumn colours all around
U mbrellas go up and down
T winkling fireworks in the sky
U nder leaves the hedgehogs lie
M y feet kick up leaves higher and higher
N ow time for a hot chocolate by the fire.

Lucy Probets (6)
East Claydon School, East Claydon

Amélie

A lways playing with my friends
M arley and Pearl are my cats
E very day I cuddle my mummy
L ovely weather makes me smile
I love my brother very much
E njoy being at school.

Amélie Prudhomme (6)
East Claydon School, East Claydon

Indigo

I am a colour of the rainbow

N ight sky sapphires

D arkest times

I nk damp, I can stamp it

G lass reflecting sun

O n water.

Luna Mae Price (6)

East Claydon School, East Claydon

Animal Family

F rogs have brothers
A nts have aunties
M oths have cousins
I guanas have fathers
L lamas have sisters
Y aks have mothers.

Maisie McIvor (6)
East Claydon School, East Claydon

Football

F antastic sport
O ptimistic we'll get the best result
O ne of the most popular sports
T allying up the points for the leaderboard
B all always in a game
A lways interactive
L aughing because they lost against a rubbish team
L onely when they get relegated.

Remy Lenehan (7)
Fingringhoe CE Primary School, Fingringhoe

Minecraft

M inecraft is my favourite game
I have found The Aether
N obody has created a world like me
E vil mobs everywhere
C louds in the sky
R ed arrows
A ngel pigs flying
F lowers blowing in the wind
T he creepers in The Aether.

Samuel Dilliway (7)
Fingringhoe CE Primary School, Fingringhoe

Bunny

B unnies like to hop as they go through the woods

U sually they like digging burrows and living in it, *dig dig*

N ormally they like eating carrots, *crunch crunch*

N ormally they are soft and fluffy

Y ummy vegetables, *mmm!*

Poppy Cockram (6)

Fingringhoe CE Primary School, Fingringhoe

Family

F amily is important for me

A lways I'm having fun playing football with my brother

M e and my brother, we nearly play games every night

I like playing games with my brother

L ove my sister

Y ummy food Mummy makes.

Alessandro Asioli (6)
Fingringhoe CE Primary School, Fingringhoe

Animals

A nimals are my favourite things
N early all animals live in the zoo
I saw a sloth at the zoo
M y animal is a pig
A pig is an animal
L eopards are my favourite animal
S ometimes guinea pigs squeal.

Renesmay Willsher (6)
Fingringhoe CE Primary School, Fingringhoe

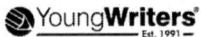
Horse

H orses are my favourite animals
O ne horse is enough but I prefer seven
R eally, my favourite one is Buck
S ally is my favourite
E veryone has sat on something beautiful.

Millie Kay Jones (6)
Fingringhoe CE Primary School, Fingringhoe

Cats

C razy, cute, cheeky, cuddly
A lways really funny
T heir tails are really long
S uper clever and cheeky.

Charlie Walker (6)

Fingringhoe CE Primary School, Fingringhoe

Watermelon

W atermelon is juicy, no wonder because it is named water

A pple pie is a bit too sweet, don't you think?

T una smells too fishy

E nergy is a bit too high

R unning like I can't anymore

M ore energy every time I eat

E nergy like Pac-Man

L ittle did I know I was going to explode if I ate some more

O range stings when you squirt it in your eyes

N o, I'm going to explode!

Lily Leigh Wells (9)
Grove CE Primary School, Grove

Wonderland

W hat a wonderful place
O nce there was magic, it was so fantastic
N ever question the fairy princess
D own where the animals lie down by the bay
E ager to dance and play
R un rabbit, run, they say
L ie down and relax
A wonderful day today
N o catching any animals from the hay
D o what you want and play.

Olivia Dalgleish (10)
Grove CE Primary School, Grove

My Family

M y family are the best you will ever get
Y ou don't even know how much I love my family.

F amilies are amazingly kind and helpful
A lovely family I have
M y family cares for me with all their heart
I love my family to bits
L ove my sister lots and lots
Y ou love your family and you know it.

Megan Zamora Rowe (9)
Grove CE Primary School, Grove

Dragons

D arted tall like a spear or even sharper

R *oar*, her roar was louder than any

"A rgh!" people scream because her face is scarier than anyone's face

G ary is her human friend that is fascinated by her

O verhead her fire breath went

N o ending fire breath

S oon there will be more...

Benny Stoten (9)

Grove CE Primary School, Grove

Camping

C ome and enjoy a night away

A nd sleep under the stars and see them shining bright

M ake a cup of tea to keep you warm

P our some sauce over barbecue sausages

I t's fun to be playing in the park

N o one worries about the time

G et into your sleeping bag, it's time to sleep.

Eleanor-May Woodley (7)
Grove CE Primary School, Grove

Halloween

H aunted houses are scary

A nd fun

L ots of fun for everyone

L oads of candy in my belly

O f chocolate and sweets aplenty

W itches come out to play

E erie ghosts say, "Boo!"

E xciting costumes are worn

N ow it's time to trick or treat, woo!

Jack Perkins (9)
Grove CE Primary School, Grove

The Vicious Tiger

T igers like meat, they are vicious and really hungry all of the time

I would like to bump into one at night-time

G irl tigers may look pretty but they are vicious like daddy tigers

E ven if the cubs look very cute, they are also vicious like their mum and dad

R eal tigers live in Africa.

Charlotte Lily Dalgleish (7)
Grove CE Primary School, Grove

Buddy Barnes

B uddy is my puppy
U sually amazing
D angerous but cute
D igging holes is his thing
Y eah, Buddy.

B est friend
A little dog
R ude to Esme
N ice, cute and fluffy
E normous love
S till amazing Buddy.

Beth Barnes (7)
Grove CE Primary School, Grove

Dolphins

D ancing dolphin in the sea
O bedient dolphins eating fish
L oving dolphins in the sea playing with humans
P eeping dolphins
H iding dolphins
I ncredible dolphins dancing
N ice dolphins watching their friends
S uper dolphins.

George Mowatt (7)
Grove CE Primary School, Grove

Maxumas

M ax is magnificent

A dorable Max

X mas is his favourite time

U sed Teddy

M e and Max have been everywhere

A lovely Teddy

S omeone who loves its owner.

Justin James Harvey Mathieson (7)

Grove CE Primary School, Grove

Jessie

J essie is very, very, very joyful
E xcited Jessie on her dinosaur
S killed Jessie
S uper Jessie to the rescue
I ncredible Jessie on her horse
E xquisite Jessie.

Annabeth Manton (7)
Grove CE Primary School, Grove

Silly Fish

S tupid a bit
I t eats flies
L ikes shrimp
L ikes people
Y awns all the time.

F abulous
I mpossible
S leepy
H andyman.

Morgan Niblett (8)
Grove CE Primary School, Grove

Roblox

R unning happily in a game
O pening game ready for me
B eating up a zombie
L oving and caring
O bbies are sometimes easy
X marks the spot of the game.

Summer Langley (8)

Grove CE Primary School, Grove

World War

W orld
O ff-road
R ationed food
L ong as six years
D anger.

W ar
A nderson shelters
R ation books.

Megan Hackwood (9)
Grove CE Primary School, Grove

My Mum

M um, I need some help
U m, I can't find my teddy
M um, I think it's in my bed, can we go and
check?
S o let's go now, can we please?

Keira Kelly (6)
Grove CE Primary School, Grove

Jesus

J esus is our father

E veryone is playing in Heaven

S aviour of all of us

U p above us is Heaven

S till loves us no matter what.

Naila Amonua Amoa-Sakyi (9)
Grove CE Primary School, Grove

Mr Cat

M eows a lot
R uns around the house.

C utest cat in the history of cats
A mazingly fast
T errifyingly cuddly.

Isaac Mattam (7)
Grove CE Primary School, Grove

My Sister Megan

M agnificent and silly

E xcellent and wonderful

G reat and kind

A mazing and loving

N egative at doing homework.

Phoebe Hackwood (7)

Grove CE Primary School, Grove

My Family

M y family are funny
Y ou can read nicely, Jack.

F airly you can work hard, Daddy
A nd you are pretty, Hope
M ummy, you are pretty
I love my family
L ooking good and pretty, Emma
Y ou are pretty, Mummy.

Evie Whitehouse (6)
Limehurst Community Primary School, Limehurst Village

Sweets

S weets are not healthy
W e know sweets are not healthy
E veryone likes sweets
E ven better with a milkshake
T hey are colourful and different shapes
S ome are tangy and tasty.

Noah James Bowden (6)

Limehurst Community Primary School, Limehurst Village

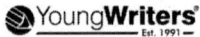

My New School

S tarting my new school, I was excited to make new friends,

C oming in every day to play, learn and pray.

H appy when I can run in the playground and play football in PE,

O livia, Alfie, Barry and Harry I love most of all in my class.

O ur favourite things to do are read books and play in the toy house,

L eaving at the end of the day to tell my family what I've done.

Cameron Poulsom (4)

St Joseph's Catholic Primary School, Aldershot

Artistic

A visit to a Disney princess is fun
R eading books is what I enjoy
T rampolining is a club I do
I like to eat pizza and cottage pie
S weets are my favourite treat
T he film Snow White is what I watch
I love swimming whenever I can
C uddling Mummy is the best.

Mary McGinty (4)
St Joseph's Catholic Primary School, Aldershot

Spaghetti

S crummy yummy

P lease can I have spaghetti?

A delicious meal

G iggle because it's slurpy

H ave it with cheese

E xtra spaghetti, please

T asty basil sprinkled on my dinner

T omato, juicy, saucy

I love spaghetti!

Ava Campbell (4)

St Joseph's Catholic Primary School, Aldershot

Rainbow

R ed school bag

A melia gave me a conker

I love reading books

N anny Mandy has a swing at her house

B oyfriend is Cameron

O livia likes teddies

W ishing a star in your heart to come.

Olivia Norman (4)

St Joseph's Catholic Primary School, Aldershot

Leopards

L ions hunt

E lephants have trunks

O ctopuses have eight legs

P anthers pounce

A nimals are cool and stick together

R hinos charge

D ogs bark

S harks bite.

Eli Barclay (4)

St Joseph's Catholic Primary School, Aldershot

Unicorn

U mbrella in my hand
N uts in my tummy
I love snow
C ats are my favourite pets
O liver is my sweet brother
R ainbow in the sky
N aughty kitty running after a mouse.

Zuzanna Witoslaw (4)
St Joseph's Catholic Primary School, Aldershot

Ava-Mary

A child
V ery good sometimes
A dancer.

M y mummy I love
A big sister
R eally clever
Y our friend.

Ava-Mary Eldred (4)
St Joseph's Catholic Primary School, Aldershot

Family

F ather
A ndreea
M ummy
I oan
L ove
Y ellow.

Andreea Vlad (4)

St Joseph's Catholic Primary School, Aldershot

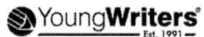

Gardening

G ardening is my favourite thing to do
A dding lots of colourful plants
R aking up the leaves
D igging out the weeds
E njoy listening to the birds
N ests in the trees
I plant vegetables
N ature is beautiful
G ardening every weekend.

Emily Ann Falby (7)
Stickney CE Primary School, Stickney

Gymnastics

G ymnastics is great

Y ou meet lots of friends

M ats laid on the floor

N ew routines

A dance to music

S tanding on the balancing beam

T ime to go home

I enjoyed my lesson

C an't wait to go back

S ee you next week!

Karlie Benton (6)
Stickney CE Primary School, Stickney

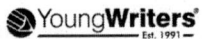
Gymnastics

G ymnastics is lots of fun
Y ou should have a go
M ats on the floor
N ever give up
A beam for me to walk on
S tanding tall on the bars
T rying not to fall
I balance on the beam
C arefully jump off
S tand like a star.

Isla Clarke (6)
Stickney CE Primary School, Stickney

Football

F ootball is fun

O n the pitch I play

O n a Saturday

T ogether we play

B low the whistle

A ll run for the ball

L et's score a goal

L et's win!

Reggie Waterson (6)

Stickney CE Primary School, Stickney

Swimming

S wimming for a team
W e have lots of fun
I love swimming
M eet lots of friends
M y fans cheer me on
I do lots of it
N ow we race
G ood, I won.

Jake Toin (6)
Stickney CE Primary School, Stickney

Reading

R eading is fun
E njoy the story
A dventures with characters
D angerous or not
I love to read
N ever want to stop
G ood books in the library.

Amelia Patching (6)
Stickney CE Primary School, Stickney

Biking

B iking is fun
I love to ride my bike
K nees are bending
I wear my helmet and knee pads
N ew bikes for my birthday
G reat fun riding my bike.

Logan Diamond (7)
Stickney CE Primary School, Stickney

Biking

B iking is fun
I like riding my bike
K nees going up and down
I wear my blue helmet
N ew, shiny bike
G oing up and down the road.

Max Morbey (7)
Stickney CE Primary School, Stickney

Dancing

D ance at my house
A nd in the kitchen
N ever stop dancing
C at joins in too
E veryone loves to dance.

Adele Smith (6)
Stickney CE Primary School, Stickney

Swimming

S wimming with my sisters
W ith my mum and dad too
I love swimming
M ermaids swim too.

Valentina Smith (6)

Stickney CE Primary School, Stickney

The Stuff I Like

J ames loves football
A wonderful league I'm in
M y mum is very sporty
E xcellent friends I have
S uper at sport.

H oovering is one of my talents
O liver is my brother
W onderful at colouring
E ngland is where I live
L iverpool is my favourite team
L iving near a beach is great.

James Howell (7)
West Kirby Primary School, West Kirby

Christmas

C arol singing

H olly wreath making

R eindeer prancing

I cicles forming

S tockings hanging

T ree decorating

M ince pies baking

A ll are waiting

S anta's coming.

Tabby Simpson (6)
West Kirby Primary School, West Kirby

Matthew

M y favourite sport is football
A ttack, defence, goal
T ackling helps the team
T ogether we can win
H appily we score
E veryone runs and cheers
W e have won the game.

Matthew Kerwick (6)
West Kirby Primary School, West Kirby

Easter

E ggs to fill your tummy

A ngels love to fly

S unday gives you time to rest

T rinity on high

E ating chocolate bunnies

R abbits jump up to the sky.

Charlotte Rowland (6)
West Kirby Primary School, West Kirby

Sharks

S cary carnivores
H unting alone
A super-fast fish
R azor-sharp teeth
K illed by people unfairly
S o misunderstood.

Philip McCormick (6)
West Kirby Primary School, West Kirby

Young Writers Information

We hope you have enjoyed reading this book – and that you will continue to in the coming years.

If you're a young writer who enjoys reading and creative writing, or the parent of an enthusiastic poet or story writer, do visit our website **www.youngwriters.co.uk**. Here you will find free competitions, workshops and games, as well as recommended reads, a poetry glossary and our blog. There's lots to keep budding writers motivated to write!

If you would like to order further copies of this book, or any of our other titles, then please give us a call or order via your online account.

Young Writers
Remus House
Coltsfoot Drive
Peterborough
PE2 9BF
(01733) 890066
info@youngwriters.co.uk

Join in the conversation!
Tips, news, giveaways and much more!

 YoungWritersUK   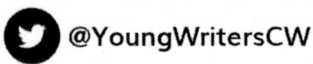 @YoungWritersCW